Midnight Quilts

11 Sparkling Projects to Light Up the Night

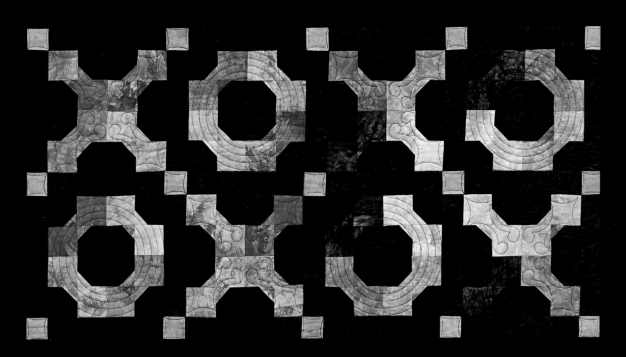

Lerlene Nevaril

C&T PUBLISHING

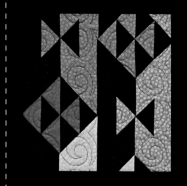
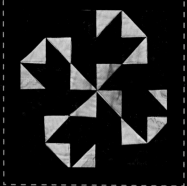

Text copyright © 2012 by Lerlene Nevaril

Photography and Artwork copyright © 2012 by C&T Publishing, Inc.

Publisher: Amy Marson

Creative Director: Gailen Runge

Acquisitions Editor: Susanne Woods

Editors: Phyllis Elving and Liz Aneloski

Technical Editors: Ellen Pahl and Alison Schmidt

Cover Designer: Kristy Zacharias

Book Designer: Kristen Yenche

Production Coordinator: Jenny Davis

Production Editor: S. Michele Fry

Illustrator: Aliza Shalit

Photography by Christina Carty-Francis and Diane Pedersen
of C&T Publishing, Inc., unless otherwise noted

Published by C&T Publishing, Inc., P.O. Box 1456, Lafayette, CA 94549

Library of Congress Cataloging-in-Publication Data

Nevaril, Lerlene, 1938-

 Midnight quilts : 11 sparkling projects to light up the night / Lerlene Nevaril.

    p. cm.

 ISBN 978-1-60705-456-6 (soft cover)

 1. Patchwork--Patterns. 2. Quilting--Patterns.
 3. Color in textile crafts. I. Title.

 TT835.N4685 2012

 746.46--dc23

                          2011034031

Printed in China

10 9 8 7 6 5 4 3 2 1

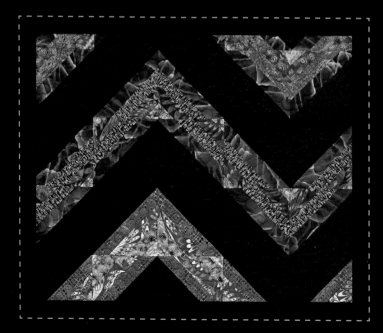

Contents

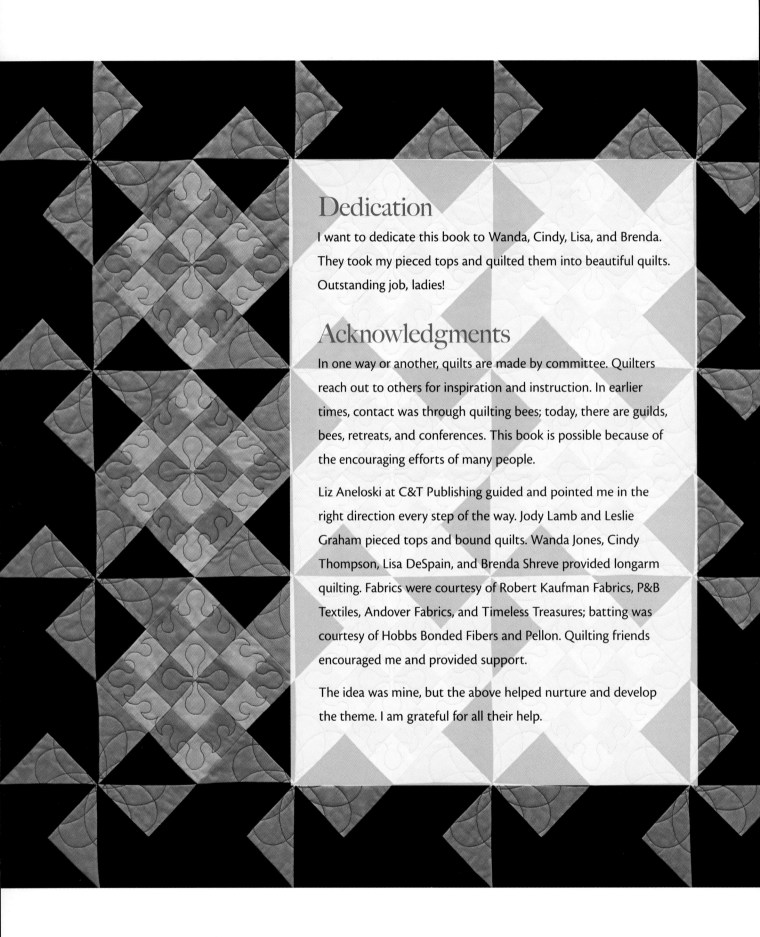

Dedication

I want to dedicate this book to Wanda, Cindy, Lisa, and Brenda. They took my pieced tops and quilted them into beautiful quilts. Outstanding job, ladies!

Acknowledgments

In one way or another, quilts are made by committee. Quilters reach out to others for inspiration and instruction. In earlier times, contact was through quilting bees; today, there are guilds, bees, retreats, and conferences. This book is possible because of the encouraging efforts of many people.

Liz Aneloski at C&T Publishing guided and pointed me in the right direction every step of the way. Jody Lamb and Leslie Graham pieced tops and bound quilts. Wanda Jones, Cindy Thompson, Lisa DeSpain, and Brenda Shreve provided longarm quilting. Fabrics were courtesy of Robert Kaufman Fabrics, P&B Textiles, Andover Fabrics, and Timeless Treasures; batting was courtesy of Hobbs Bonded Fibers and Pellon. Quilting friends encouraged me and provided support.

The idea was mine, but the above helped nurture and develop the theme. I am grateful for all their help.

Introduction

Thumb through a stack of the latest quilt magazines and quilt books and you will see an interesting trend developing. The featured quilts are more dark than light. But these quilts aren't dark and drab; rather, they are dark and bright. Quilters are discovering that bright colors "pop" better against dark fabrics than they do against light fabrics.

The same 1930s reproduction fabrics are used for both of these quilts. The difference?
The design on the left has a white and light-colored background, and the one on the right has a black background.

See how much more vibrant and bright the 1930s fabrics look against black than against the pale background in the examples at right. That this is not really something new is evident when one looks back at yesterday's quilts. We have wonderful examples made by Amish quilters in the nineteenth and early twentieth centuries. These quilts were made primarily with bright and deeply saturated colors and black; a light-colored background was extremely rare. At the turn of the twentieth century many quilters made crazy quilts, another style with an emphasis on black to make the other colors shine. Let's not forget the primitive wool penny rugs of the 1800s; once again, black was the color of choice to frame the "pennies." Many of the Log Cabin quilts from the nineteenth century combine black with bright colors for contrast. One of the first quilts I made in the 1980s was a Double Wedding Ring—with a black background.

Black backgrounds with up-to-date fabrics give all these quilts a contemporary flair. They are dramatic. They are bright. They are fun!

This book presents patterns for eleven quilts, plus a gallery of a baker's dozen more to show the dramatic effects you can achieve by using dark backgrounds to create remarkable quilts. It includes patterns for every skill level, from beginner to advanced; make these quilts to advance your skill level or simply to have fun—or both.

So expand your horizons! Take a break from the everyday, and see how black can add extra sparkle to your quilts.

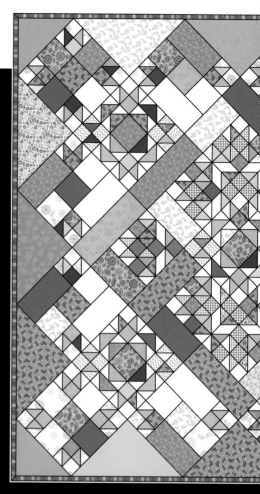

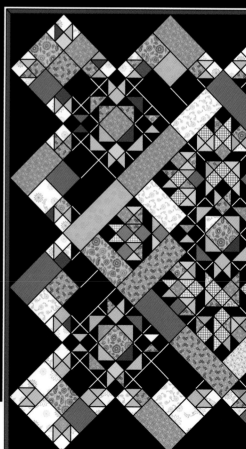

The basic techniques used for the quilts throughout this book are presented here. It's important to take the time to read through these instructions before you begin any of the projects.

Materials and Cutting

The quilts included in the book illustrate the wide range of fabrics that can be enhanced and intensified by combining them with black: batiks, hand-dyes, '30s prints, Japanese designs, contemporary patterns, tone-on-tones, the Fossil Fern line by Benartex, and prints by Kaffe Fassett, to name a few.

Yardage requirements given for all the quilts are based on a usable fabric width of 40". All cutting includes ¼" seam allowances.

Piecing

All block sizes and measurements for the projects are based on using an accurate ¼" seam allowance. Press all seams after sewing, in the direction indicated by the arrows in the how-to illustrations.

SEW-AND-FLIP TECHNIQUE

Using this technique, you do not need to actually cut any triangles. Triangular patches are created from squares and rectangles.

1. Place the 2 pieces, usually a square and a rectangle, right sides together, aligning the raw edges as indicated for the individual project. Draw a diagonal line from corner to corner on the wrong side of the small square.

2. Sew along the marked line. Trim away the fabric outside the stitching to leave a ¼" seam allowance and flip open the top piece; press.

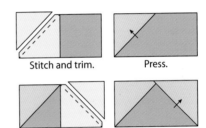

Stitch and trim.   Press.

The first fabric layers must be trimmed before you add a second square on top, as some designs require. Refer to the specific project diagrams for other piecing variations that use this basic technique.

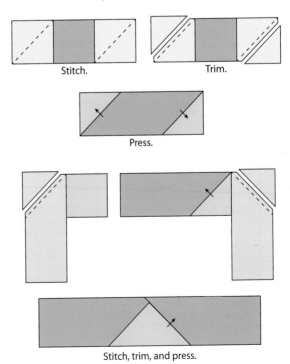

Stitch.   Trim.

Press.

Stitch, trim, and press.

HALF-SQUARE TRIANGLES

These units are made from pairs of squares. In the cutting charts for the projects, these are the squares with measurements ending in $\frac{7}{8}$".

1. Place 2 squares right sides together with the lighter color on top, carefully aligning all raw edges. Draw a diagonal line from corner to corner.

2. Stitch $\frac{1}{4}$" from the drawn line on both sides, creating a double seam. Cut apart on the line. Open the squares and press the seams toward the darker triangles.

Stitch. Cut. = Press.

Setting Triangles

Quilts that call for on-point settings need triangles to fill in the sides and corners when the blocks are set diagonally into rows. To make these, cut squares and then cut them diagonally in quarters (for side triangles) or halves (for corner triangles). The triangles are cut slightly larger than needed, to allow for piecing variances and to ensure a good fit. When the quilt top is completely assembled, trim and square up the outside edges of your quilt, leaving an accurate $\frac{1}{4}$" seam allowance.

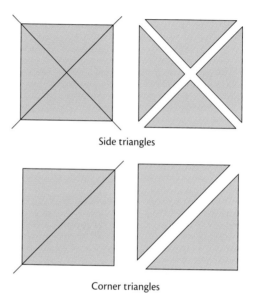

Side triangles

Corner triangles

Attaching Borders

Border strips for the quilts are cut on the crosswise grain to conserve fabric, so sometimes they will need to be pieced. Borders are cut longer than you will actually need to allow for any piecing differences. The yardage listed allows for borders to be cut crosswise and pieced for the most efficient use of fabric. For some quilts, you will have enough yardage to cut borders either way, but to be safe, purchase extra fabric for lengthwise cutting.

First, measure the length of the assembled quilt top through the center of the quilt. Trim the side border strips to match, and sew them to the quilt sides. Next, measure the quilt width through the center of the quilt, including the newly added side borders. Trim the top and bottom border strips to fit and sew in place. Repeat the measuring and cutting process if the quilt has additional borders. Unless the project instructions specify otherwise, press the border seams away from the center of the quilt.

If you are adding corner squares, measure the length and width of the quilt top through the center. Cut the side, top, and bottom borders to fit, and stitch the side borders in place. Sew the corner squares to the ends of the top and bottom borders, and then sew these borders to the quilt.

Backing, Batting, and Binding

The backing and batting measurements for the projects in this book extend 4″ beyond the quilt dimensions on all sides. This is to allow for piecing differences and also to provide for ease in quilting. Prepare the backing by cutting and piecing to the required dimensions.

The binding strips for most of the quilts are cut 2¼″ wide for double-fold binding. This will give you a binding that finishes at approximately ⅜″ wide. Follow these steps to bind your finished quilt top:

1. Sew the binding strips together, using diagonal seams, to make a single long strip. Press the seams open.

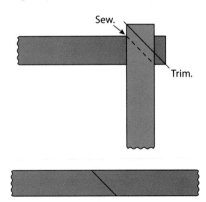

2. Fold and press the strip in half lengthwise, wrong sides together and raw edges even.

3. With raw edges aligned, stitch the binding to the front of the quilt, using a ¼″ seam and leaving the first few inches of the binding unattached.

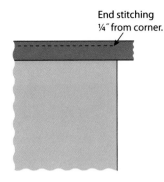

4. Stop ¼″ away from the first corner and backstitch one stitch. Lift the presser foot and needle. Rotate the quilt one-quarter turn and fold the binding up at a right angle so that it extends above the quilt and forms a 45° angle. Fold the binding strip down, even with the edge of the quilt, and begin sewing at the folded edge. Repeat this step at each corner.

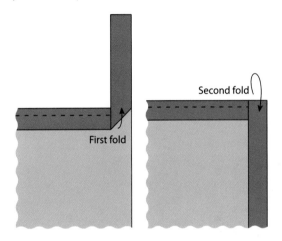

5. Continue stitching until you are a few inches from the beginning of the binding strip. Lay the ending strip over the beginning strip. Overlap the 2 strips by the cut width of the binding (usually 2¼″) and trim the ending strip. Open both ends of the binding and place them right sides together at a right angle. Sew diagonally across the ends. Trim the seam to ¼″ and press open. Refold the binding and finish stitching.

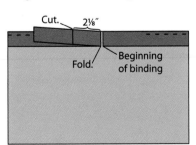 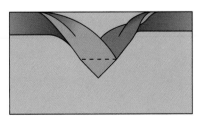

6. Turn the binding to the back of the quilt and hand sew the folded edge in place on the seamline, using a blind stitch and mitering the corners as you reach them. Match your thread to the binding, not the backing fabric.

Whirligigs

Designed and pieced by Lerlene Nevaril,
machine quilted by Wanda Jones, 2009

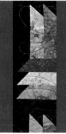

This quilt offers the perfect opportunity to use all those
beautiful batiks you can't stop buying for your stash. Just 24
strips of fabric, 2″ × 40″ each, plus your chosen focus fabric
and black background material, make up the quilt. Red is the
focus fabric in this quilt, but your whirligig centers could just
as easily be blue, green, or any other color you prefer.

Finished quilt: 48½″ × 60½″

Finished blocks: 12″ × 12″

Setting: Horizontal 3 × 4

Materials and Cutting | Based on 40" fabric width

FABRIC	YARDAGE	USED FOR	NUMBER TO CUT	SIZE TO CUT
BRIGHT FOCUS FABRIC	⅔ yard	Blocks, piece A; Border 2; binding	53 rectangles	2" × 6½"
ASSORTED BRIGHT COLORS	1½ yards total or 24 strips 2" × 40"	Blocks, piece B; Border 2; binding	136 rectangles	2" × 6½"
BLACK	2⅔ yards	Blocks, piece C	48 rectangles	2" × 6½"
		Blocks, piece D	144 squares	2" × 2"
		Border 1	2 strips	2" × 52"*
			2 strips	2" × 43"*
		Border 3	2 strips	3½" × 58"*
			2 strips	3½" × 52"*
		Binding	6 strips	2" × fabric width
BACKING	3⅛ yards			
BATTING	56" × 68"			

Cut the border strips lengthwise or cut them crosswise and piece to this length as necessary.

tips

Batiks are undeniably beautiful, but working with these tightly woven fabrics can be a challenge. Here are some steps you can take to minimize problems:

- *When pinning, use the thinnest, sharpest pins you can find.*

- *Use a microtex rather than a universal needle in your sewing machine; this needle, with its slender shaft and sharp point, more easily pierces the tight weave of batiks.*

- *If you are having trouble sewing straight or you hear your needle "punching" through the layers, change the needle so that you keep working with a very sharp point.*

Making the Blocks

Follow the steps below to make 12 blocks, pressing the seams as indicated by the arrows in the illustrations.

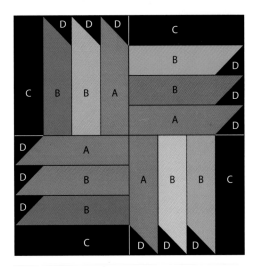

1. Make 48 units using pieces A and D and the sew-and-flip technique (page 7).

Make 48.

2. Make 96 units using pieces B and D.

Make 96.

3. Sew units from Steps 1 and 2 together with the C pieces to make 48 units as shown. Make sure that A (the focus fabric) is always on the bottom and C (black) is always on the top. Vary the placement of the B fabrics so that they will be randomly distributed in the final blocks.

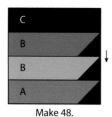

Make 48.

4. Assemble and stitch 12 blocks, using 4 units from Step 3 for each block and orienting the units as shown. Arrange the units so that the B fabrics are randomly distributed.

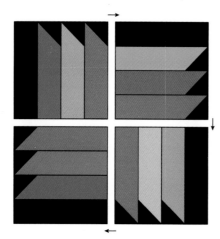

Assembling the Quilt

Arrange the blocks into 4 rows of 3 blocks each according to the assembly diagram (page 13). Sew the blocks together in rows. Press the seams in opposite direction from row to row. Sew the rows together, pressing the seams all in the same direction.

ADDING BORDERS

Press the seams toward the black borders after each step.

1. Measure the length of the quilt top through the center of the quilt. Trim the 2″ × 52″ black borders to fit. Sew to the quilt sides.

2. Measure the width of the quilt top through the center of the quilt, including the border strips you just attached. Trim the 2″ × 43″ black borders to fit. Sew to the top and bottom of the quilt.

3. Join an A piece and 10 B pieces end to end using diagonal seams to make a side border strip. Make 2 strips. Measure the quilt from top to bottom through the center, including Border 1, and trim the strips to fit. Sew to the sides of the quilt.

4. Join an A piece and 8 B pieces end to end using diagonal seams to make a border strip. Make 2 strips. Measure the quilt top from side to side through the center, including both borders, and trim the strips to fit. Sew them to the top and bottom of the quilt.

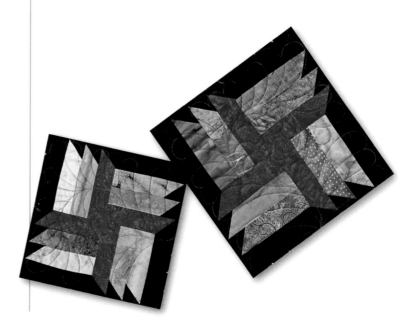

5. Using the 3½″ × 58″ black strips for the sides of the quilt and the 3½″ × 52″ black strips for the top and bottom, measure, trim, and attach the same as for Border 1.

Assembly diagram

Finishing the Quilt

1. Layer and pin or baste the quilt top, batting, and backing. Quilt as desired.

2. Sew the remaining 2″ × 6½″ colored rectangles between the black binding strips using diagonal seams. Prepare and attach the binding (see page 9).

---
tip

Let's talk about bindings. The main purpose of the binding is to enclose and protect the raw edges of the quilt. It is also your last chance to make a design statement.

The binding on **Whirligigs** *has 6″ color inserts—a subtle and unexpected touch.* **Beyond the Grid** *(page 19) has a pieced border, with the binding made from the same fabrics.* **Summer Vegetable Patch** *(page 61), with its black sashing and border, needed color and pattern in its binding to frame the quilt. The binding on* **Lanterns in the Garden** *(page 57) is a slightly darker green than the border, giving a subtle but elegant finish to the quilt.*

Conclusion: It's worth taking the time to choose a binding that will take your quilt up a notch.

Wyoming Valley

Designed by Lerlene Nevaril, pieced by Jody Lamb,
machine quilted by Wanda Jones, 2010

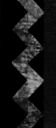

Although this looks like an on-point setting, *Wyoming Valley* actually consists of horizontally set blocks within three borders. Carrying colors across block lines and into the first border creates an optical illusion of larger blocks set on the diagonal.

Finished quilt: 60½″ × 60½″

Finished blocks: 12″ × 12″

Setting: Horizontal 3 × 3

Select light, medium, and dark values of 5 different colors. Colors 1, 2, 3, and 4 are for the blocks in the corners of the quilt; color 5 is for the center block. I used fuchsia, violet, blue, and red for colors 1–4 and orange for color 5.

FABRICS	YARDAGE	USED FOR	NUMBER TO CUT	SIZE TO CUT
DARK COLORS 1, 2, 3, 4	¼ yard of each	Block 1, piece A	4 squares of each	2½" × 2½"
		Border 2, corner square	1 square of each	4½" × 4½"
MEDIUM COLORS 1, 2, 3, 4	⅛ yard of each	Block 1, piece B	6 squares of each	2⅞" × 2⅞"
LIGHT COLORS 1, 2, 3, 4	⅜ yard of each	Block 1, piece C	4 rectangles of each	2½" × 4½"
		Block 1, piece D	8 squares of each	2½" × 2½"
		Block 2, piece B	2 rectangles of each	2½" × 4½"
		Block 2, piece C	4 squares of each	2½" × 2½"
		Border 1, piece A	2 rectangles of each	2½" × 4½"
		Border 1, piece D	4 squares of each	2½" × 2½"
DARK COLOR 5	⅛ yard	Block 1, piece A	4 squares	2½" × 2½"
MEDIUM COLOR 5	⅛ yard	Block 1, piece B	6 squares	2⅞" × 2⅞"
LIGHT COLOR 5	½ yard	Block 1, piece C	4 rectangles	2½" × 4½"
		Block 1, piece D	8 squares	2½" × 2½"
		Block 2, piece B	4 rectangles	2½" × 4½"
		Block 2, piece C	8 squares	2½" × 2½"
DARK GREEN	1⅛ yards	Block 2, piece A	16 squares	2½" × 2½"
		Border 2, piece A	44 rectangles	2½" × 4½"
		Border 2, piece B	88 squares	2½" × 2½"
LIGHT GREEN	⅜ yard	Block 2, piece B	4 rectangles	2½" × 4½"
		Block 2, piece C	8 squares	2½" × 2½"
		Border 1, piece A	4 rectangles	2½" × 4½"
		Border 1, piece D	8 squares	2½" × 2½"
BLACK	4½ yards	Block 1, piece E	5 squares	4½" × 4½"
		Block 1, piece F	30 squares	2⅞" × 2⅞"
		Block 1, piece G	60 squares	2½" × 2½"
		Block 1, piece H	20 rectangles	2½" × 4½"
		Block 2, piece D	20 squares	4½" × 4½"
		Block 2, piece E	32 squares	2½" × 2½"
		Block 2, piece F	16 rectangles	2½" × 4½"
		Border 1, piece B	24 squares	2½" × 2½"
		Border 1, piece C	12 rectangles	2½" × 4½"
		Border 1, piece E	12 rectangles	4½" × 8½"
		Border 1, piece F	4 squares	4½" × 4½"
		Border 2, piece C	44 rectangles	2½" × 4½"
		Border 2, piece D	88 squares	2½" × 2½"
		Border 3	2 strips	4½" × 54"*
		Border 3	2 strips	4½" × 62"*
		Binding	7 strips	2¼" × fabric width
BACKING	4 yards			
BATTING	68" × 68"			

Cut the border strips lengthwise or cut them crosswise and piece to this length as necessary.

Making the Blocks

This quilt includes 2 different block patterns. Block 1 is Wyoming Valley, and Block 2 is a "hidden" block derived by simplifying the Wyoming Valley block. Press seams as indicated by the arrows in the diagrams.

BLOCK 1

Follow the steps below to make a single block. Repeat the process for each of the 5 color families.

1. Make 12 half-square triangle units (see page 8) using pieces B and F.

Make 12.

2. Sew 3 units made in Step 1 with a G square, as shown. Make 4.

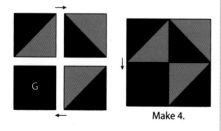

Make 4.

3. Make 1 unit for the center of the block using pieces A and E and the sew-and-flip technique (page 7).

Make 1.

4. Make 4 Flying Geese units with pieces G and C using the sew-and-flip technique.

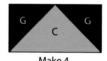

Make 4.

5. Repeat Step 4 using pieces D and H.

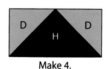

Make 4.

6. Sew together the Flying Geese units from Steps 4 and 5 as shown. Make 4.

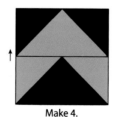

Make 4.

7. Arrange the units as shown and stitch the block together.

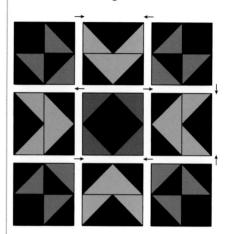

BLOCK 2

1. Make 4 units from pieces A and D as shown, using the sew-and-flip technique (page 7).

Make 4.

2. Using the sew-and-flip technique, make Flying Geese as shown. Make 4 units with light green; 4 units with color 5; and 2 units each with colors 1, 2, 3, and 4.

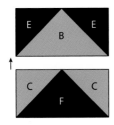

3. Make 4 blocks. In each block, place color 5 at the top of the block, light green at the bottom, and colors 1–4 at the sides as shown to match the adjacent Block 1 colors.

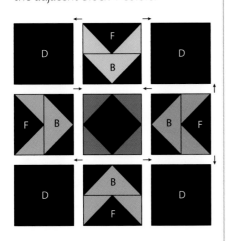

Make 1 of each.

Assembling the Quilt

Sew the blocks into horizontal rows according to the placement diagram below, placing each Block 1 in the correct position for the color sequence. Add each Block 2 so that the colors match the adjacent Block 1 colors. Press the seams in opposite directions from row to row. Sew the rows together, pressing all the seams in one direction.

Block placement diagram

Adding Borders

Add the borders one at a time, pressing the seams toward Borders 1 and 3.

BORDER 1

1. Using the sew-and-flip technique (page 7), make 2 units each for colors 1, 2, 3, and 4. Make 4 units with light green.

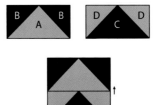

Make 2 of colors 1–4.
Make 4 of light green.

2. Arrange units from Step 1 with black E and F pieces as shown to make left and right border strips. Attach to the sides of the pieced quilt center, checking that the colors of the units in the border match the colors of the adjacent blocks in the quilt center.

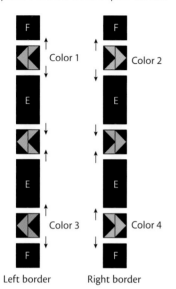

Left border   Right border

3. Arrange units from Step 1 with black E pieces as shown to make the top and bottom borders. Stitch to the quilt, checking that the colors of the units in the border match the colors of the adjacent blocks in the quilt center.

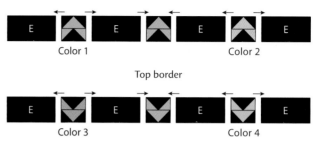

Top border

Bottom border

BORDER 2

1. Make 44 Flying Geese units with the A and D border pieces and 44 with the B and C pieces using the sew-and-flip technique (page 7).

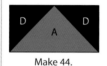 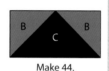

Make 44.   Make 44.

2. Make 44 units by joining the Step 1 units.

Make 44.

3. Combine 11 of the Step 2 units into a row. Make 4 rows. Sew a row to the right and left sides of the quilt.

4. For the top row, sew a color 1 corner square to the left end of a border row and a color 2 corner square to the right end. Sew to the top of the quilt. For the bottom row, sew a color 3 corner square to the left end of the remaining border row and a color 4 corner square to the right end. Sew to the bottom of the quilt.

— note: —
Each corner square should match the color of the adjacent Block 1.

BORDER 3

1. Measure the quilt length, including the first 2 borders, through the center of the quilt. Trim the 4½" × 54" strips to match and sew to the sides of the quilt.

2. Measure the quilt width, including borders, through the center of the quilt. Trim the 4½" × 62" strips to match, and sew to the top and bottom of the quilt.

Assembly diagram

Finishing the Quilt

1. Layer and pin or baste the quilt top, batting, and backing. Quilt as desired.

2. Prepare the binding (see page 9), and bind the quilt edges.

Designed and pieced by Lerlene Nevaril,
machine quilted by Wanda Jones, 2011

Beyond the Grid

Finished quilt: 55½" × 70½"

Finished blocks: 13" × 13"

Setting: Horizontal 3 × 4

This quilt is a study in illusion. The illusion is that large fabric squares are framed by narrow black bands and overlaid by wider black bands. To create this illusion, pieces are cut from fat quarters, separated into different quilt blocks, and then arranged and sewn together so that the fabrics are back in their original orientations.

A smaller version of this pattern, *Summer Vegetable Patch* (page 61), is made from vegetable-print fabrics. Other theme prints you might consider include sports, animals, flowers, musical instruments, cars and trucks, and sewing motifs.

Materials and Cutting | Based on 40″ fabric width

The fabric requirements were simplified to incorporate 20 different fat quarters, but feel free to use fewer fat quarters and duplicate a couple of them as in the quilt shown. Before you cut, assign letters to each fabric. Refer to the block layout guide (page 21) to help label the fabrics. You may want to choose your favorites for F, G, J, K, N, and O. When cutting the fat quarters, refer to the cutting diagram (page 21). If you have a directional print, be sure to keep the block pieces oriented correctly.

FABRIC	YARDAGE	USED FOR	NUMBER TO CUT	SIZE TO CUT
1 PRINT: A	1 fat quarter (18″ × 22″)	Block 1	1 rectangle	4½″ × 8½″
		Blocks 1–12*	12 squares	1½″ × 1½″
		Sashing squares*	20 squares	2½″ × 2½″
		Border	1 square	4½″ × 4½″
			1 rectangle	4½″ × 8½″
		Binding	1 strip	2¼″ × 15″
5 PRINTS: B, C, H, L, P	1 fat quarter of each	Blocks 1, 2, 3, 6, 9	1 square from each	4½″ × 4½″
			1 rectangle from each	4½″ × 8½″
		Border	1 square from each	4½″ × 4½″
			1 rectangle from each	4½″ × 8½″
		Binding	1 strip from each	2¼″ × 15″
1 PRINT: D	1 fat quarter	Block 3	1 square	4½″ × 4½″
		Border	1 square	4½″ × 4½″
			1 rectangle	4½″ × 8½″
		Binding	1 strip	2¼″ × 15″
5 PRINTS: E, I, M, R, S	1 fat quarter of each	Blocks 1, 4, 7, 10, 11, 12	1 square from each	8½″ × 8½″
			1 rectangle from each	4½″ × 8½″
		Border	1 square from each	4½″ × 4½″
			1 rectangle from each	4½″ × 8½″
		Binding	1 strip from each	2¼″ × 15″
6 PRINTS: F, G, J, K, N, O	1 fat quarter of each	Blocks 1–12	1 square from each	4½″ × 4½″
			2 rectangles from each	4½″ × 8½″
			1 square from each	8½″ × 8½″
		Border	1 square from each	4½″ × 4½″
			1 rectangle from each	4½″ × 8½″
		Binding	1 strip from each	2¼″ × 15″

FABRIC	YARDAGE	USED FOR	NUMBER TO CUT	SIZE TO CUT
1 PRINT: Q	1 fat quarter	Block 10	1 square	8½" × 8½"
		Border	1 square	4½" × 4½"
			1 rectangle	4½" × 8½"
		Binding	1 strip	2¼" × 15"
1 PRINT: T	1 fat quarter	Block 12	1 rectangle	4½" × 8½"
		Border	1 square	4½" × 4½"
			1 rectangle	4½" × 8½"
		Binding	1 strip	2¼" × 15"
BLACK	1½ yards	Blocks 1–12	24 rectangles	1½" × 4½"
			24 rectangles	1½" × 8½"
		Sashing	31 strips	2½" × 13½"
BACKING	3⅝ yards			
BATTING	64" × 78"			

*The small squares for the blocks and the sashing squares can be cut from fabrics D, Q, or T, if desired.

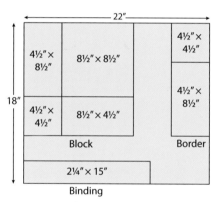

Cutting diagram for fat quarters

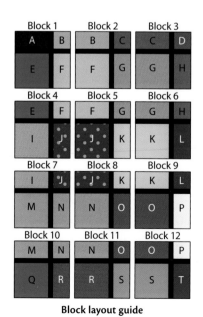

Block layout guide

Making the Blocks

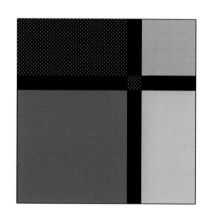

1. Beginning with Block 1 in the upper left corner, sew the 4 block pieces, the 1½" black rectangles, and the 1½" square together as shown. Each of the 4 main block fabrics will be different.

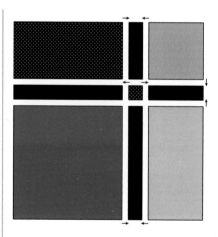

2. Repeat to piece Blocks 2–12.

— *tip* —

Number each block in the upper left corner as you complete it (using the numbers on the block layout guide). This will make it easier to assemble the blocks and sashing in the quilt top.

Assembling the Quilt

Sew the blocks into rows with the 2½″ black sashing strips. Sew the sashing rows with the dark print 2½″ sashing squares, referring to the assembly diagram (below). Check the order and orientation of your blocks while sewing. If the blocks are not placed in the right order, with the correct colors on top, the grid pattern will be lost.

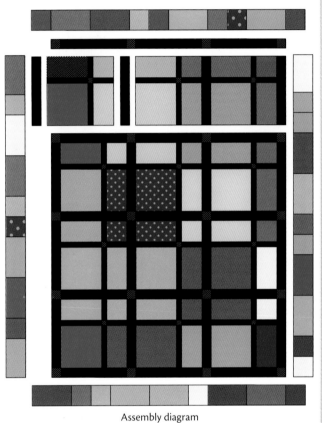

Assembly diagram

ADDING THE BORDER

1. Sew the border squares and rectangles into strips as shown, placing the different fabrics as desired.

2. See Attaching Borders (page 8) for instructions on measuring the quilt top and attaching the side borders first and then the top and bottom borders.

tip

Each border strip will be slightly longer than needed. After measuring your quilt, trim equal amounts from each end to fit.

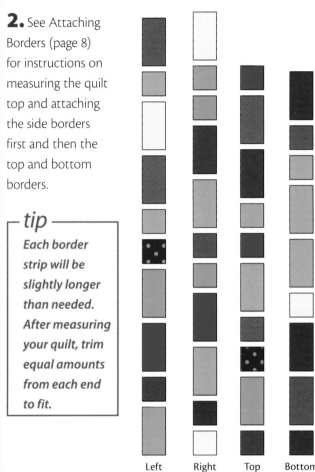

Left border   Right border   Top border   Bottom border

Finishing the Quilt

1. Layer and pin or baste the quilt top, batting, and backing. Quilt as desired.

2. Prepare the binding (page 9), piecing the strips together with straight seams. Bind the quilt.

tip

By using straight seams to join the binding strips, the binding seams will echo the straight seams used in the pieced borders.

Designed and pieced by Lerlene Nevaril,
machine quilted by Cindy Thompson, 2011

Twirling Pinwheels

Finished quilt: 57¾" × 57¾"

Finished blocks: 8" × 8"

Setting: On point 4 × 4

You can almost feel these fanciful pink and blue pinwheels twirling above the vibrant checkerboard background of this quilt. Neon-bright colors add to the sense of motion.

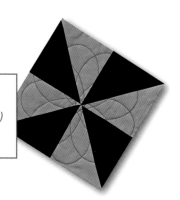

tip

To make this same design as a very easy and scrappy quilt, use precut 2½″ strips for the 16-Patch blocks and use a layer cake square (10″ × 10″) to cut each of the Pinwheel blocks.

 Materials and Cutting | Based on 40″ fabric width

FABRICS	YARDAGE	USED FOR	NUMBER TO CUT	SIZE TO CUT
PINK	¾ yard	Pinwheel blocks, piece A	8 squares	4⅞″ × 4⅞″
		Border 1	2 strips	2½″ × 52″*
			2 strips	2½″ × 48″*
BLUE	1 yard	Pinwheel blocks, piece A	24 squares	4⅞″ × 4⅞″
		16-Patch blocks, piece A	72 squares	2½″ × 2½″
LIME GREEN	½ yard	16-Patch blocks, piece B	72 squares	2½″ × 2½″
BLACK	2¾ yards	Pinwheel blocks, piece B	32 squares	4⅞″ × 4⅞″
		Side setting triangles	3 squares	13¾″ × 13¾″; cut in quarters diagonally to make 12 triangles
		Corner setting triangles	2 squares	7½″ × 7½″; cut in half diagonally to make 4 triangles
		Border 2	2 strips	4½″ × 52″*
			2 strips	4½″ × 62″*
		Binding	6 strips	2¼″ × fabric width
BACKING	3⅔ yards			
BATTING	65″ × 65″			

*Cut the border strips crosswise and piece to this length.

Making the Blocks

PINWHEEL BLOCKS

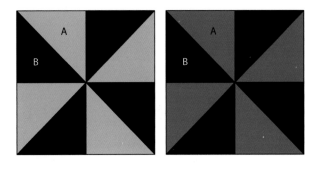

Follow Steps 1–4 to make 4 pink Pinwheel blocks and 12 blue Pinwheel blocks.

1. Make 16 half-square triangle units (see page 8) using the 8 pink A pieces and the 8 black B pieces.

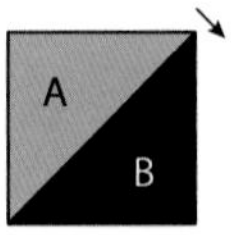

2. Sew the half-square triangle units together to make 4 pink blocks as shown.

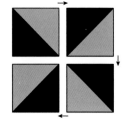

3. Repeat Step 1 to make 48 half-square triangle units using the 24 blue A pieces and 24 black B pieces.

4. Sew the half-square triangle units together as shown to make 12 blue blocks.

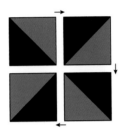

16-PATCH BLOCKS

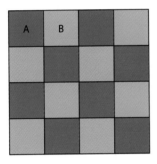

Sew 8 blue A squares and 8 lime green B squares together as shown in the diagram. Press seams in the direction of the arrows. Make 9 blocks.

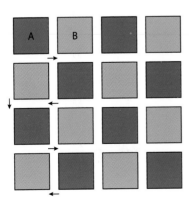

Assembling the Quilt

1. Sew the blocks and setting triangles in diagonal rows as indicated in the assembly diagram. Press the seams in opposite directions from row to row. Note that the setting triangles were cut slightly oversized for easier assembly.

2. Trim the outer edges to a ¼" seam allowance beyond the block points.

ADDING BORDERS

Press the seams away from the center of the quilt after each step.

1. Measure the length of the quilt top through the center. Trim the 2½" × 48" pink border strips to match and sew them to the sides of the quilt.

2. Measure the width of the quilt through the center, including the pink borders. Trim the 2½" × 52" pink border strips to match and sew to the top and bottom of the quilt.

3. Measure the quilt length through the center, including the pink border. Trim the 4½" × 52" black strips to match and sew them to the sides of the quilt.

4. Measure the width of the quilt through the center, including the pink and black borders. Trim the 4½" × 62" black strips to match and sew to the top and bottom of the quilt.

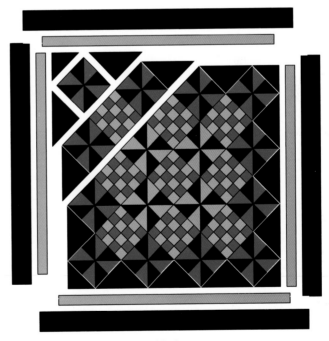

Assembly diagram

Finishing the Quilt

1. Layer and pin or baste the quilt top, batting, and backing. Quilt as desired.

2. Prepare the binding (see page 9), and bind the quilt edges.

Rainbow Mountains

Designed and pieced by Lerlene Nevaril,
machine quilted by Wanda Jones, 2011

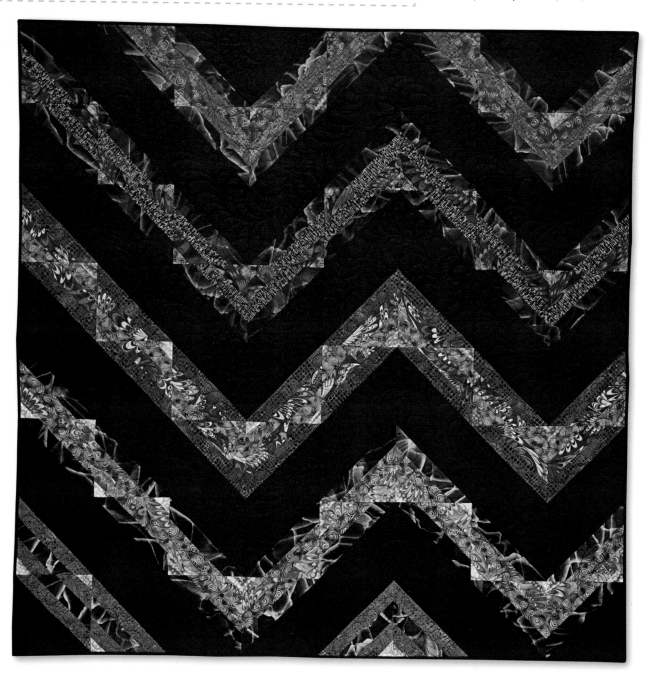

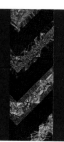

These "mountains" feel three-dimensional thanks to the choice
of fabric patterns and the light-to-dark gradation of shades
within the different color families.

Finished quilt: 64½" × 64½"

Finished blocks: 8" × 8"

Setting: Horizontal 8 × 8

Materials and Cutting

Based on 40" fabric width

You will need 5 different colors of fabrics, each in 4 shades: dark, medium, medium light, and light. The quilt shown uses red, purple, blue, green, and olive green, but have fun choosing your own favorites.

FABRICS	YARDAGE	USED FOR	NUMBER TO CUT	SIZE TO CUT
RED, DARK	⅜ yard	Blocks, piece A	11 rectangles	2" × 13"
RED, MEDIUM	⅜ yard	Blocks, piece B	11 rectangles	2" × 10"
RED, MEDIUM LIGHT	¼ yard	Blocks, piece C	11 rectangles	2" × 7"
RED, LIGHT	⅛ yard	Blocks, piece D	11 rectangles	2" × 3½"
PURPLE, DARK	½ yard	Blocks, piece A	16 rectangles	2" × 13"
PURPLE, MEDIUM	⅜ yard	Blocks, piece B	16 rectangles	2" × 10"
PURPLE, MEDIUM LIGHT	⅜ yard	Blocks, piece C	16 rectangles	2" × 7"
PURPLE, LIGHT	¼ yard	Blocks, piece D	16 rectangles	2" × 3½"
BLUE, DARK	½ yard	Blocks, piece A	16 rectangles	2" × 13"
BLUE, MEDIUM	⅜ yard	Blocks, piece B	16 rectangles	2" × 10"
BLUE, MEDIUM LIGHT	⅜ yard	Blocks, piece C	16 rectangles	2" × 7"
BLUE, LIGHT	¼ yard	Blocks, piece D	16 rectangles	2" × 3½"
GREEN, DARK	½ yard	Blocks, piece A	16 rectangles	2" × 13"
GREEN, MEDIUM	⅜ yard	Blocks, piece B	16 rectangles	2" × 10"
GREEN, MEDIUM LIGHT	⅜ yard	Blocks, piece C	16 rectangles	2" × 7"
GREEN, LIGHT	¼ yard	Blocks, piece D	16 rectangles	2" × 3½"
OLIVE, DARK	¼ yard	Blocks, piece A	5 rectangles	2" × 13"
OLIVE, MEDIUM	¼ yard	Blocks, piece B	5 rectangles	2" × 10"
OLIVE, MEDIUM LIGHT	⅛ yard	Blocks, piece C	5 rectangles	2" × 7"
OLIVE, LIGHT	⅛ yard	Blocks, piece D	5 rectangles	2" × 3½"
BLACK	2¾ yards	Blocks, piece E	32 squares	9" × 9"; cut in half diagonally to make 64 triangles
		Binding	7 strips	2¼" × fabric width
BACKING	4 yards			
BATTING	72" × 72"			

Making the Blocks

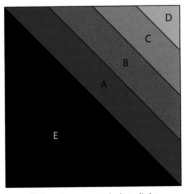

Color placement, dark to light

1. Using the dark, medium, medium-light, and light red pieces, fold each strip in half end to end and lightly press with your fingers. Fold a black triangle in half to mark the center of the long edge.

2. Sew the rectangles to a black triangle in the order shown, beginning with dark red. Use the folds to center each rectangle. Finger-press each seam away from the triangle as you sew. After all the rectangles are added, press the seams with your iron. Make 11 red blocks.

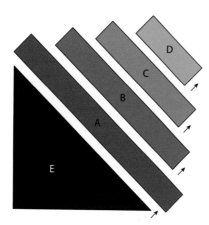

3. Repeat the process to make 16 blocks each for purple, blue, and green. Make 5 olive blocks.

4. Trim and square up each block to 8½" × 8½" with a square ruler. Place the ruler over the block so that the 8½" mark along the top and right sides of the ruler intersects the seamline between the black E triangle and the A rectangle. Trim the uneven edges along the side and top. Rotate the block 180° and trim the remaining sides of the block.

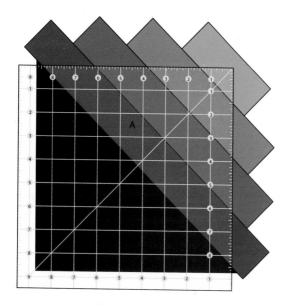

tip

The pieced edges of this block are all bias. After the blocks are trimmed, handle them carefully to avoid stretching the edges. These edges are subject to stretching until the quilt is quilted.

Assembling the Quilt

1. Arrange the blocks into 8 horizontal rows of 8 blocks each, rotating the blocks to create the design as shown in the assembly diagram.

2. Sew the blocks into horizontal rows. Press the seams in opposite directions from row to row.

3. Sew the rows together to complete the quilt top. Press all the seams between rows in the same direction.

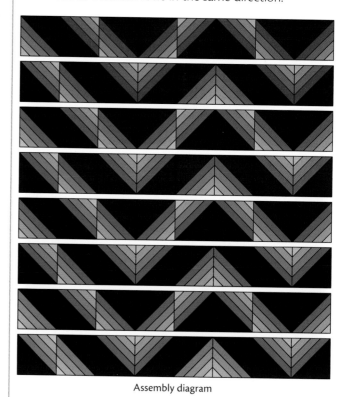

Assembly diagram

Finishing the Quilt

1. Layer and pin or baste the quilt top, batting, and backing. Quilt as desired.

2. Prepare the binding (see page 9), and bind the quilt edges.

Designed by Lerlene Nevaril, pieced by Leslie Graham,
machine quilted by Cindy Thompson, 2011

Finished quilt: 46″ × 46″

Finished blocks: 8″ × 8″

Setting: Horizontal 4 × 4

Bow ties in four colors form stylized X's and O's, like a whimsical, oversized tic-tac-toe board—or a generous offering of hugs and kisses!

Choose 4 different colors of fabric in 4 values: light, medium light, medium, and dark. The quilt shown includes pink, green, purple, and blue. Yellow sashing squares add rays of sunshine.

FABRICS	YARDAGE	USED FOR	NUMBER TO CUT	SIZE TO CUT
PINK: light, medium light, medium, and dark	¼ yard of each	Blocks, piece A	8 squares from each	2½″ × 2½″
		Blocks, piece B	8 squares from each	1½″ × 1½″
GREEN: light, medium light, medium, and dark	¼ yard of each	Blocks, piece A	8 squares from each	2½″ × 2½″
		Blocks, piece B	8 squares from each	1½″ × 1½″
PURPLE: light, medium light, medium, and dark	¼ yard of each	Blocks, piece A	8 squares from each	2½″ × 2½″
		Blocks, piece B	8 squares from each	1½″ × 1½″
BLUE: light, medium light, medium, and dark	¼ yard of each	Blocks, piece A	8 squares from each	2½″ × 2½″
		Blocks, piece B	8 squares from each	1½″ × 1½″
BLACK	2¼ yards	Blocks, piece C	128 squares	2½″ × 2½″
		Sashing	40 rectangles	2″ × 8½″
		Border	2 strips	3½″ × 42″*
			2 strips	3½″ × 48″*
		Binding	5 strips	2¼″ × fabric width
YELLOW	¼ yard	Sashing squares	25 squares	2″ × 2″
BACKING	3 yards			
BATTING	54″ × 54″			

Cut the border strips lengthwise or cut them crosswise and piece to this length as necessary.

Making the Blocks

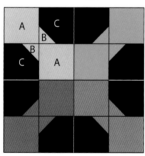

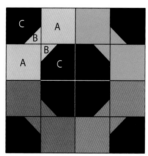

1. Make 32 units as shown with the black C squares and the pink B squares, using the sew-and-flip technique (page 7). Make 8 from each shade of pink.

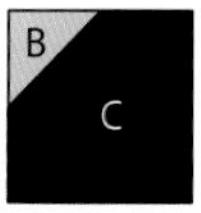

Make 8.

2. Using the Step 1 units and the pink A squares, make 16 Bow Tie blocks—4 from each shade of each of pink.

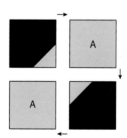

3. Sew 1 light, 1 medium light, 1 medium, and 1 dark Bow Tie block together as shown to make an "X" block. Make 2 blocks.

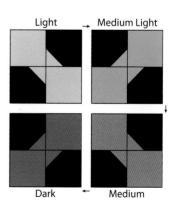

4. Sew 1 light, 1 medium light, 1 medium, and 1 dark Bow Tie block together as shown to make an "O" block. Make 2 blocks.

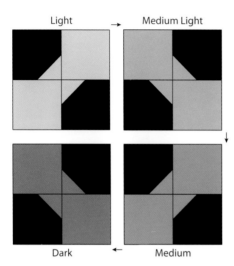

Light → Medium Light

Dark ← Medium

5. Repeat Steps 1–4 for green, purple, and blue.

Assembling the Quilt

1. Refer to the assembly diagram to arrange the blocks into 4 horizontal rows of 4 blocks each. Add sashing strips and corner squares between the blocks. Turn the blocks so that the light bow ties in each colorway are in the center of the grouping, as shown in the color placement diagram.

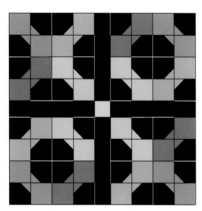

Color placement diagram

2. Sew the blocks and sashing strips into rows. Sew the sashing strips and corner squares into rows. Press all seams toward the sashing strips.

3. Sew the rows together to complete the quilt top.

Assembly diagram

ADDING THE BORDER

1. Measure the length of the quilt top through the center. Trim the 3½" × 42" border strips to match and sew to the sides of the quilt.

2. Measure the width of the quilt top through the center, including the borders. Trim the 3½" × 48" border strips to match and sew to the top and bottom of the quilt.

Finishing the Quilt

1. Layer and pin or baste the quilt top, batting, and backing. Quilt as desired.

2. Prepare the binding (see page 9), and bind the quilt edges.

Nighttime Sky

Designed and pieced by Lerlene Nevaril,
machine quilted by Wanda Jones, 2011

The more fabrics you use to make the nine-patches for your quilt, the more sparkle it will have. I used 28 different fabrics in this quilt.

Finished quilt: 41½″ × 41½″

Finished blocks: 9″ × 9″

Setting: Horizontal 3 × 3

Materials and Cutting

Based on 40″ fabric width

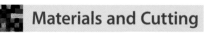

FABRICS	YARDAGE	USED FOR	NUMBER TO CUT	SIZE TO CUT
VARIETY OF BRIGHT FABRICS	1 yard total	Nine-patch units, center block, Border 2, piece A	28 strips	1½″ × 20″
		Log Cabin block, piece A	8 squares	1½″ × 1½″
		Log Cabin block, piece C	8 rectangles	1½″ × 3½″
		Log Cabin block, piece E	8 rectangles	1½″ × 5½″
		Log Cabin block, piece G	8 rectangles	1½″ × 7½″
		Log Cabin block, piece I	4 rectangles	1½″ × 9½″
BLUE	1⅜ yards	Center block, piece D	1 square	5½″ × 5½″
		Border 1	2 strips	1½″ × 29″
			2 strips	1½″ × 31″
		Border 3	2 strips	3½″ × 38″*
			2 strips	3½″ × 44″*
		Binding	5 strips	2¼″ × fabric width
BLACK	1¼ yards	Nine-patch units, center block, Border 2, piece B	26 strips	1½″ × 20″
		Double Nine-Patch block, piece C	16 squares	3½″ × 3½″
		Center block, piece C	4 rectangles	2½″ × 3½″
		Log Cabin block, piece B	8 rectangles	1½″ × 2½″
		Log Cabin block, piece D	8 rectangles	1½″ × 4½″
		Log Cabin block, piece F	8 rectangles	1½″ × 6½″
		Log Cabin block, piece H	8 rectangles	1½″ × 8½″
BACKING	2¾ yards			
BATTING	49″ × 49″			

Cut the border strips lengthwise or cut them crosswise and piece to this length as necessary.

Making the Blocks

The first step in making this quilt is to sew the nine-patch units that will be used for the Double Nine-Patch blocks, center block, and Border 2. You will have extra units. This will enable you to achieve a pleasing distribution of color and patterns throughout the quilt.

tip

Use the extra nine-patch units to make a companion pillow, or use them to make an interesting pieced backing.

NINE-PATCH UNITS

1. Make 10 strip sets by sewing a 20″ black strip between 2 of the bright strips. Cut each strip set into 13 segments, 1½″ wide. These will be the ABA segments.

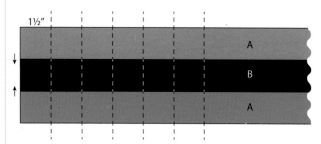

2. Make 8 strip sets by sewing a 20″ bright strip between 2 black strips. Cut each strip set into 13 segments, 1½″ wide. These will be the BAB segments.

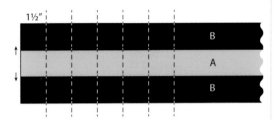

DOUBLE NINE-PATCH BLOCKS

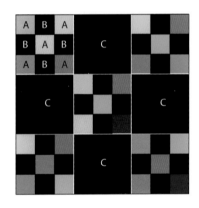

1. Make 20 nine-patch units by sewing 2 ABA segments to a BAB segment as shown.

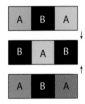

2. Make 4 Double Nine-Patch blocks using 5 nine-patch units from Step 1 and 4 of the C pieces in each.

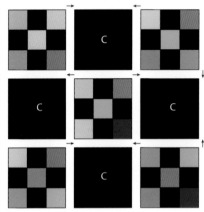

CENTER BLOCK

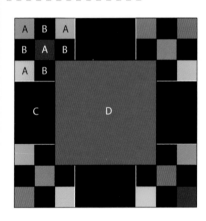

1. Make 2 units as shown, using ABA and BAB segments and a black C rectangle.

2. Remove a square from 4 of the strip set segments and sew together with a black C rectangle to make 2 units as shown.

3. Make the center block by sewing together the Step 1 units, the Step 2 units, and the D square.

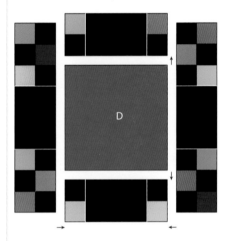

LOG CABIN BLOCKS

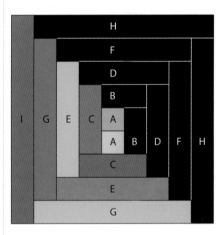

1. Sew 2 bright A squares together for the block center.

2. Add rectangles to the Step 1 unit in alphabetical order and in a counter-clockwise direction, ending with piece I.

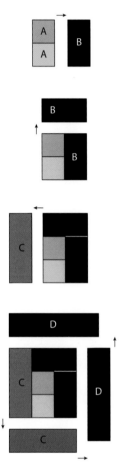

3. Repeat the steps to make 4 Log Cabin blocks.

Assembling the Quilt

Refer to the assembly diagram to arrange the blocks into 3 horizontal rows of 3 blocks each. Sew the blocks into rows. Press the seams in opposite directions from row to row. Sew the rows together to complete the quilt top.

BORDER 1

1. Measure the quilt length through the center of the quilt. Trim the 1½" × 29" blue strips to match. Sew to the sides of the quilt.

2. Measure the width of the quilt through the center. Trim the 1½" × 31" blue strips to match. Sew to the top and bottom of the quilt. Press the seams toward Border 1.

BORDER 2

1. Sew together 14 ABA segments alternately with 15 BAB segments, beginning and ending with BAB. Make 2 strips and sew to the sides of the quilt.

2. Alternate 18 ABA segments with 17 BAB segments, beginning and ending with ABA. Make 2 strips and sew to the top and bottom of the quilt. Press the seams toward Border 1.

BORDER 3

1. Measure the length of the quilt through the center, including the first 2 borders. Trim the 3½" × 38" blue strips to match. Sew to the sides of the quilt.

2. Measure the width of the quilt through the center, including the borders. Trim the 3½" × 44" blue strips to match. Sew to the top and bottom of the quilt. Press the seams toward Border 3.

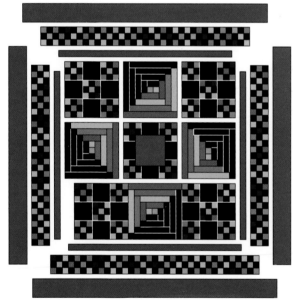

Assembly diagram

Finishing the Quilt

1. Layer and pin or baste the quilt top, batting, and backing. Quilt as desired.

2. Prepare the binding (see page 9), and bind the quilt edges.

Bear's Paw Beauty

Designed and pieced by Lerlene Nevaril,
machine quilted by Wanda Jones, 2011

Brilliant blossoms formed by Bear's Paw blocks almost seem to jump off the black background of this quilt garden. Rich blue borders, echoing the blossom colors, intensify the effect.

Finished quilt: 72″ × 72″

Finished blocks: 14″ × 14″

Setting: On point 3 × 3

Materials and Cutting | Based on 40″ fabric width

Each Bear's Paw block is made from 3 shades of a single color. Two blocks each are made from colors 1, 2, 3, and 4. One block is made from color 5. The 4 Hidden Paw blocks are all made from 2 shades of blue. The same yellow fabric is used for the centers of all the blocks.

FABRICS	YARDAGE	USED FOR	NUMBER TO CUT	SIZE TO CUT
DARK, colors 1–4	¼ yard of each	Bear's Paw block, piece A	16 squares from each	2½″ × 2½″
MEDIUM, colors 1–4	¼ yard of each	Bear's Paw block, piece B	16 squares from each	2½″ × 2½″
LIGHT, colors 1–4	¼ yard of each	Bear's Paw block, piece C	16 squares from each	2⅞″ × 2⅞″
DARK, color 5	⅛ yard	Bear's Paw block, piece A	8 squares	2½″ × 2½″
MEDIUM, color 5	⅛ yard	Bear's Paw block, piece B	8 squares	2½″ × 2½″
LIGHT, color 5	⅛ yard	Bear's Paw block, piece C	8 squares	2⅞″ × 2⅞″
DARK BLUE	1¾ yards	Hidden Paw block, piece A	16 squares	2½″ × 2½″
		Border 2	4 strips	4½″ × 66″*
		Binding	8 strips	2¼″ × fabric width
MEDIUM BLUE	1 yard	Hidden Paw block, piece B	16 squares	2⅞″ × 2⅞″
		Border 1	4 strips	2½″ × 62″*
YELLOW	⅜ yard	Bear's Paw block, piece D	9 squares	2½″ × 2½″
		Hidden Paw block, piece C	4 squares	2½″ × 2½″
		Border 1, corner square	4 squares	2½″ × 2½″
		Border 2, corner square	4 squares	4½″ × 4½″
BLACK	3½ yards	Bear's Paw block, piece E	36 rectangles	2½″ × 6½″
		Bear's Paw block, piece F	36 squares	2½″ × 2½″
		Bear's Paw block, piece G	72 squares	2⅞″ × 2⅞″
		Hidden Paw block, piece D	16 rectangles	2½″ × 4½″
		Hidden Paw block, piece E	16 squares	2⅞″ × 2⅞″
		Hidden Paw block, piece F	16 squares	2½″ × 2½″
		Hidden Paw block, piece G	8 rectangles	2½″ × 10½″
		Hidden Paw block, piece H	8 rectangles	2½″ × 14½″
		Side setting triangles	2 squares	22¼″ × 22¼″; cut in quarters diagonally to make 8 triangles
		Corner setting triangles	2 squares	11¾″ × 11¾″; cut in half diagonally to make 4 triangles
BACKING	4½ yards			
BATTING	80″ × 80″			

Cut the border strips crosswise and piece to this length.

Making the Blocks

BEAR'S PAW BLOCK

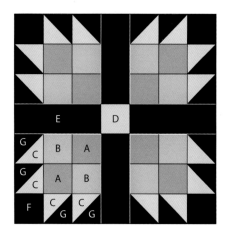

1. Using black G pieces and the C pieces from colors 1–4, make 32 half-square triangle units (see page 8) for each color. Make 16 half-square triangle units with the C pieces of color 5 and the black G pieces.

2. Sew 4 units from Step 1 together with pieces A, B, and F as shown. Make 8 units each for colors 1–4. Make 4 units for color 5.

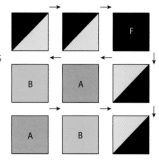

3. Arrange 4 units from Step 2 together with 4 black E pieces and 1 yellow D square as shown. Sew together to make a block. Make 2 blocks each for colors 1–4. Make 1 block for color 5.

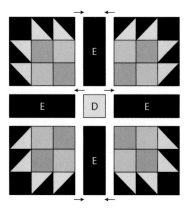

HIDDEN PAW BLOCK

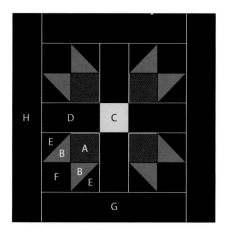

1. Using medium blue B pieces and black E pieces, make 32 half-square triangle units (see page 8).

Make 32.

2. Sew 2 units from Step 1 together with the A and F pieces to make 16 units as shown.

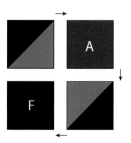

3. Make 4 blocks using the Step 2 units and the C, D, G, and H pieces as shown.

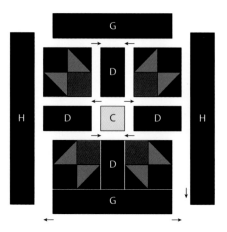

Assembling the Quilt

1. Arrange the blocks and setting triangles in diagonal rows as shown in the assembly diagram. Sew the blocks into rows. Press the seams in opposite directions from row to row. Sew the rows of blocks together to complete the quilt top. Note that the setting triangles were cut slightly oversized for easier assembly.

2. Trim the quilt center, leaving a ¼" seam allowance beyond the block points.

ADDING BORDERS

1. Measure the quilt through the center, top to bottom and side to side. Trim the 4 medium blue 2½" × 62" strips to match. Sew border strips to the right and left sides of the quilt.

2. Sew a 2½" yellow square to each end of the remaining 2 medium blue strips; then sew the strips to the top and bottom of the quilt.

3. Measure the quilt length and width through the center. Trim the 4 dark blue 4½" × 66" strips to match. Sew strips to the right and left sides of the quilt.

4. Sew a 4½" yellow square to each end of the remaining 2 dark blue strips; then sew the strips to the top and bottom of the quilt.

Assembly diagram

Finishing the Quilt

1. Layer and pin or baste the quilt top, batting, and backing. Quilt as desired.

2. Prepare the binding (see page 9) and bind the quilt edges.

One Color Quilt shows how you can interpret the design for *Bear's Paw Beauty* in a single hue to create a completely different look.

Spiral Star Table Runner

Designed and pieced by Lerlene Nevaril,
machine quilted by Brenda Shreve, 2011

This runner introduces a star block with sharply angled triangles that create elegant radiating star points. Using a dark warm red for the stars creates depth, and mixing a variety of black fabrics for the background adds texture.

Finished table runner: 22½″ × 46½″

Finished blocks: 6″ × 6″

Setting: Horizontal 3 × 7

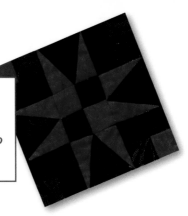

tip

This runner and the two that follow are made with the same general layout. You can swap any 6″ pieced or appliquéd block for those shown. Substitute flower, leaf, heart, tree, pumpkin, house, and bunny blocks to make a year's worth of table runners.

Materials and Cutting

Based on 40″ fabric width

FABRICS	YARDAGE	USED FOR	NUMBER TO CUT	SIZE TO CUT
RED	1⅓ yards	Star block, piece A	2 strips	1½″ × fabric width
		Star block, piece C	44 triangles	Template C (page 43)
		Star block, piece Cr	44 triangles	Template Cr (page 43)
		Border	2 strips	2½″ × 44″
			2 strips	2½″ × 24″
		Binding	4 strips	2¼″ × fabric width
BLACKS (approximately 6 different blacks)	1¼ yards total	Star block, piece B	8 strips	1½″ × fabric width
		Star block, piece D	44 triangles	Template D (page 43)
		Nine-Patch block, piece A	6 strips	2½″ × fabric width
BACKING	1½ yards			
BATTING	30″ × 54″			

Making the Blocks

STAR BLOCK

1. Make 2 strip sets using the 1½″ red and black strips. Cut into 44 segments 1½″ wide.

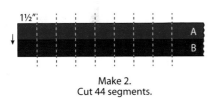

Make 2.
Cut 44 segments.

2. Make 3 strip sets from the remaining 1½″ black strips. Cut into 66 segments 1½″ wide.

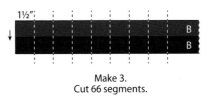

Make 3.
Cut 66 segments.

3. Make 11 four-patch units by sewing together pairs of Step 1 segments.

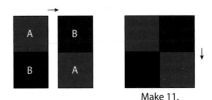

Make 11.

4. Make 22 four-patch units by sewing together a red-and-black segment from Step 1 and an all-black segment from Step 2.

Make 22.

5. Make 22 all-black four-patch units by sewing together pairs of Step 2 segments.

Make 22.

6. Make 44 units by sewing together patches cut with templates C, Cr, and D as shown. (See the tip box at right for helpful hints.)

Make 44.

7. Make 11 blocks by arranging the units from Steps 3–6 as shown.

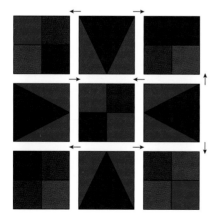

NINE-PATCH BLOCK

1. Make 2 strip sets, using 3 black 2½" strips for each one. Cut into 30 segments 2½" wide.

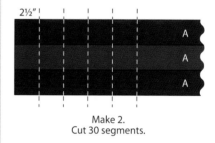

Make 2.
Cut 30 segments.

2. Sew 3 strip segments from Step 1 to make a block. Make 10 blocks.

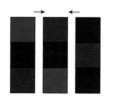

Make 10.

Assembling the Table Runner

1. Refer to the assembly diagram to sew the blocks into horizontal rows—4 rows with 2 star blocks and 1 Nine-Patch block, and 3 rows with 1 star block and 2 Nine-Patch blocks. Press the seams in each row toward the Nine-Patch blocks. Sew the rows of blocks together as shown to complete the top.

2. Measure the length of the runner through the center and trim the 2½″ × 44″ border strips to match. Sew to the sides of the runner.

3. Measure the width of the runner through the center, including the borders, and trim the 2½″ × 24″ border strips to match. Sew to the top and bottom of the runner.

Finishing the Table Runner

1. Layer and pin or baste the top, batting, and backing. Quilt as desired.

2. Prepare the binding (see page 9), and bind the edges of the runner.

Assembly diagram

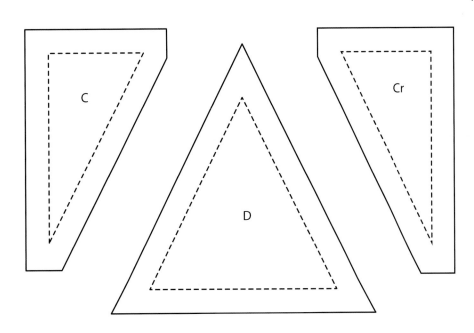

Friendship Star Table Runner

Designed and pieced by Lerlene Nevaril,
machine quilted by Cindy Thompson, 2011

Single-color stars shimmer in the black sky of this table runner. Use several different black fabrics to give your background a sense of dimension.

Finished table runner: 22½" × 46½"

Finished blocks: 6" × 6"

Setting: Horizontal 3 × 7

Materials and Cutting

Based on 40″ fabric width

FABRICS	YARDAGE	USED FOR	NUMBER TO CUT	SIZE TO CUT
PURPLE	1 yard	Star block, piece A	10 squares	2½″ × 2½″
		Star block, piece B	20 squares	2⅞″ × 2⅞″
		Border	2 strips	2½″ × 44″
			2 strips	2½″ × 24″
		Binding	4 strips	2¼″ × fabric width
BLACKS (approximately 6 different blacks)	1 yard total	Star block, piece C	20 squares	2⅞″ × 2⅞″
		Star block, piece D	40 squares	2½″ × 2½″
		Nine-Patch block, piece A	6 strips	2½″ × fabric width
			9 squares	2½″ × 2½″
BACKING	1½ yards			
BATTING	30″ × 54″			

Making the Blocks

STAR BLOCK

1. Make 40 half-square triangle units (see page 8) using the B and C squares.

Make 40.

2. Make 10 blocks by combining units from Step 1 with A and D squares as shown.

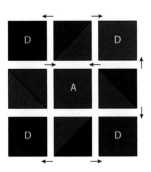

NINE-PATCH BLOCK

1. Make 10 blocks from the black strip sets, following the instructions for the Nine-Patch block (page 42).

2. Make an additional block using the 9 black A squares.

Assembling the Table Runner

1. Refer to the assembly diagram to sew the blocks into horizontal rows.

2. Measure the length of the runner through the center and trim the 2½″ × 44″ border strips to match. Sew to the sides of the runner.

3. Measure the width of the runner at the center, including the borders, and trim the 2½″ × 24″ border strips to match. Sew to the top and bottom of the runner.

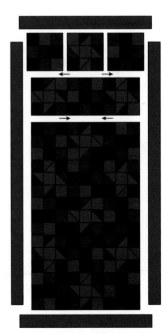

Assembly diagram

Finishing the Table Runner

1. Layer and pin or baste the top, batting, and backing. Quilt as desired.

2. Prepare the binding (see page 9), and bind the runner edges.

Christmas Lattice Table Runner

Designed and pieced by Lerlene Nevaril, machine quilted by Lisa DeSpain, 2011

We quilters love to have special pieces that we can bring out at holiday time! This runner will set a festive mood on any tabletop.

Finished table runner: 22½″ × 46½″

Finished blocks: 6″ × 6″

Setting: Horizontal 3 × 7

Materials and Cutting

Based on 40" fabric width

FABRICS	YARDAGE	USED FOR	NUMBER TO CUT	SIZE TO CUT
GREEN	⅞ yard	Lattice block, piece A	10 squares	2½" × 2½"
		Border	2 strips	2½" × 44"
			2 strips	2½" × 24"
		Binding	4 strips	2¼" × fabric width
RED	¼ yard	Lattice block, piece B	4 strips	1½" × fabric width
BLACKS (approximately 6 different blacks)	1 yard total	Lattice block, piece C	4 strips	1½" × fabric width
		Lattice block, piece D	40 squares	2½" × 2½"
		Nine-Patch block, piece A	6 strips	2½" × fabric width
			9 squares	2½" × 2½"
BACKING	1½ yards			
BATTING	30" × 54"			

Making the Blocks

LATTICE BLOCK

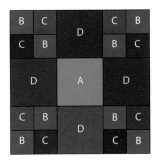

1. Make 4 strip sets using the red and black B and C strips. Cut them into 80 segments 1½" wide.

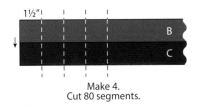

Make 4.
Cut 80 segments.

2. Make 40 units by combining the Step 1 segments as shown.

Make 40.

3. Make 10 blocks using the Step 2 units, the green A squares, and the black D squares.

NINE-PATCH BLOCK

1. Make 10 blocks from black strip sets, following instructions for the Nine-Patch block (page 42).

2. Make an additional block using the 9 black A squares.

Assembling the Table Runner

1. Refer to the assembly diagram to sew the blocks into horizontal rows, alternating rows that have 1 Lattice block with rows that have 2 Lattice blocks.

2. Measure the quilt length through the center and trim the 2½" × 44" border strips to match. Sew to the sides of the runner.

3. Measure the quilt width, including the borders, through the center and trim the 2½" × 24" border strips to match. Sew to the top and bottom of the runner.

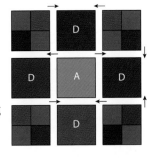

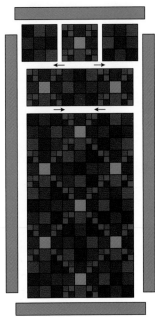

Assembly diagram

Finishing the Table Runner

1. Layer and pin or baste the top, batting, and backing. Quilt as desired.

2. Prepare the binding (see page 9), and bind the edges.

Gallery

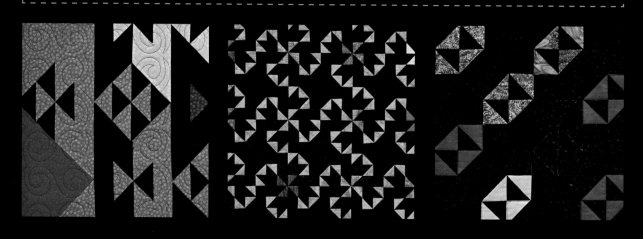

# of Quilts

Oriental Odyssey, 69½″ × 86½″, designed by Lerlene Nevaril, pieced by Leslie Graham, machine quilted by Wanda Jones, 2011

What a dramatic quilt! The black background makes the Asian fabrics glow. The green triangles give the impression that the center of the quilt is floating on top of an outer border.

Southwest Medallion, 45½" × 45½", designed and pieced by Lerlene Nevaril, machine quilted by Cindy Thompson, 2011

The colors of the Southwest give this quilt a primitive feeling. Color placement and the use of 60° angles add to the sense of a circular motif in the center of the quilt.

Something's Missing, 46½″ × 50½″, designed and pieced by Lerlene Nevaril, machine quilted by Lisa DeSpain, 2010

The "something missing" here is the trio of Broken Dishes blocks. Extra sparkle and interest in this design come from the size variation in the fabric designs, particularly the large pattern of the blue inner border and the subdued, marbelized red print.

Kaffe's Stripes, 61" × 61",
designed and pieced by Lerlene Nevaril,
machine quilted by Wanda Jones, 2009

The black background intensifies the rich, deep colors in the Kaffe Fassett fabrics used in this quilt. The use of a stripe for the setting triangles and the outer border adds interest. By cutting the setting triangles and the outer border in the same direction, and by mitering the border, the two units appear to be one. Stripes are fun to work with because they can be manipulated to produce exciting effects.

Wild and Crazy Stars, 44½″ × 44½″, designed and pieced by Lerlene Nevaril, machine quilted by Wanda Jones, 2007

This could be called a strip quilt. All the pieces, including the background, were cut from 2½″ strips. The solid centers of the Friendship Star blocks were pieced from four 2½″ squares. The original design included a 4″-wide unpieced outer border; for this quilt, it was made from the 2½″ strips pieced together.

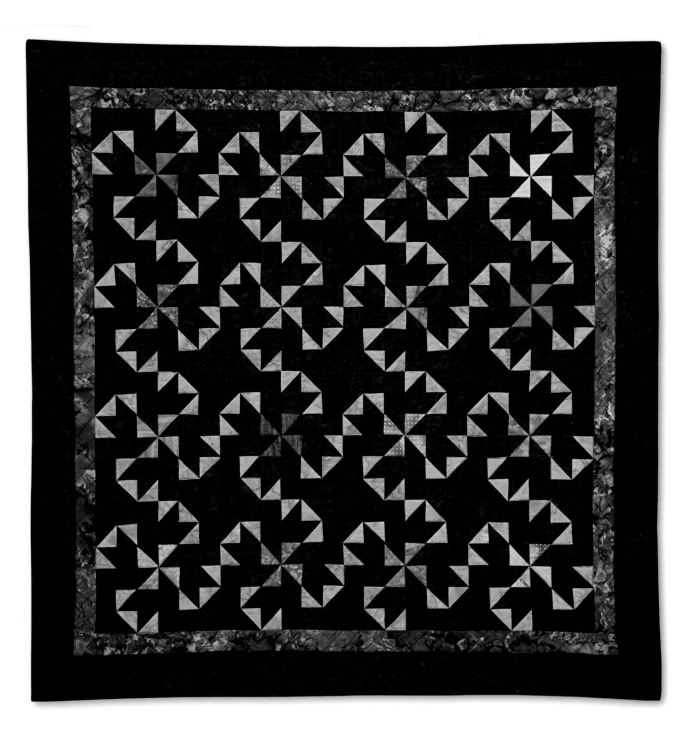

Oklahoma Twister, 45½″ × 45½″,
designed and pieced by Lerlene Nevaril,
machine quilted by Lisa DeSpain, 2011

Batiks add a shimmering quality to this quilt. The green triangles twist
and turn as though tossed by a springtime tornado over a flower bed.

Lady of the Lake, 66½″ × 66½″, designed and pieced by Lerlene Nevaril, machine quilted by Wanda Jones, 2011

When pieced using black and bright colors, the Lady of the Lake blocks give the appearance of baskets, so Wanda quilted flowers in the large colored triangles and leaves in the large black triangles.

Color on the Loose, 46″ × 57½″, designed by Lerlene Nevaril, pieced by Leslie Graham and Lerlene Nevaril, machine quilted by Cindy Thompson, 2011

Bright colors in the blocks and also in the setting triangles give this quilt a lot of energy. The black binding contains and controls it all.

Lanterns in the Garden, 69" × 69", designed and pieced by Lerlene Nevaril, machine quilted by Wanda Jones, 2011

Gold-embellished fabrics convey the impression of lanterns strung up in the garden, giving out soft light for a nighttime party.

Floral Fantasy, 79″ × 79″,
designed and pieced by Lerlene Nevaril,
machine quilted by Wanda Jones, 2011

Sashing is a great way to increase the size of a quilt without doing a lot of extra piecing. Using two colors—for the sashing and the corner squares—adds further dimension to this quilt.

Abby's Log Cabin, 42½" × 42½",
designed and pieced by Lerlene Nevaril,
machine quilted by Cindy Thompson, 2011

Log Cabin quilts made from black and small prints were found on many nineteenth-century beds. Substitute flannel in bright colors, an unusual setting, and feathers quilted with variegated thread, and this quilt is very twenty-first century.

Color Play, 56½" × 56½", designed and pieced by Lerlene Nevaril, machine quilted by Lisa DeSpain, 2011

Eight sets of light and dark fabrics make up the sixteen blocks in this quilt. Light and dark are rotated for variety. Gold in the fabrics and the quilting elevates this simple design.

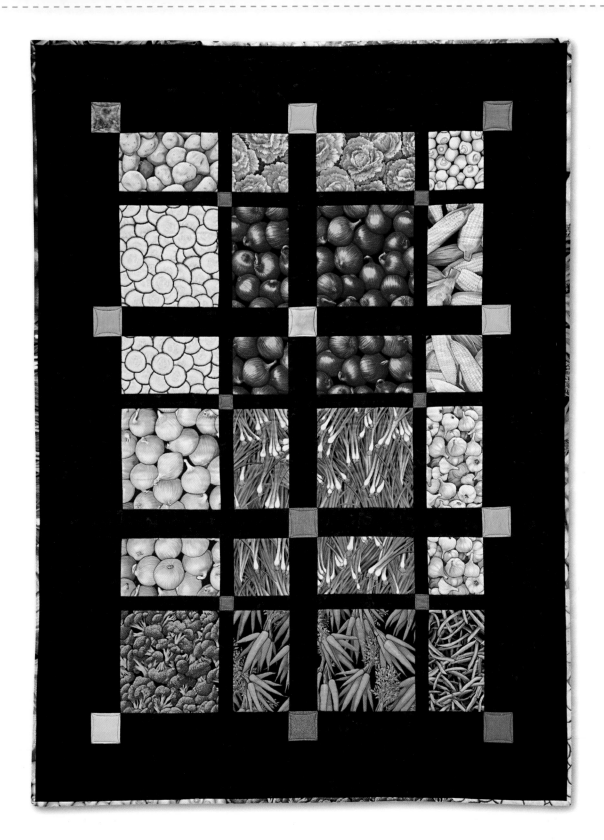

Summer Vegetable Patch, 38½″ × 52½″, designed and pieced by Lerlene Nevaril, machine quilted by Cindy Thompson, 2011

Veggie fabrics make a fun quilt. Quilting stitches outline the vegetables, and a binding made with veggie fabric strips adds a playful finishing touch. For another version of this quilt, see *Beyond the Grid*, page 19.

Resources

FABRIC

Andover Fabrics
www.andoverfabrics.com
1384 Broadway, Suite 1500
New York, NY 10018

P&B Textiles
www.pbtex.com
1580 Gilbreth Rd.
Burlingame, CA 94010

Robert Kaufman Fabrics
www.robertkaufman.com
129 West 132nd St.
Los Angeles, CA 90061

Timeless Treasures
www.ttfabrics.com
483 Broadway
New York, NY 10013

BATTING

Hobbs Bonded Fibers
www.hobbsbondedfibers.com
200 S. Commerce Dr.
Waco, TX 76710

Pellon/Legacy
www.quiltlegacy.com
4241 31st St. North
St. Petersburg, FL 33714

TRIANGULATIONS DISC

Bear Paw Productions
www.bearpawproductions.com
P.O. Box 230589
Anchorage, AK 99523

TRIANGLES ON A ROLL

HQS Inc.
www.trianglesonaroll.com
P.O. Box 94237
Phoenix, AZ 85070

QUILTING SOFTWARE

Electric Quilt Company
www.electricquilt.com
419 Gould St., Suite 2
Bowling Green, OH 43402

LONGARM MACHINE QUILTING

Cindy Thompson, Chrome Top Quilts
620-331-9300
email: chrometopquilts@tvecwb.com

Lisa DeSpain, My Modern Quilts
www.mymodernquilts.com
918-232-6155
email: quiltmaster@mymodernquilts.com

Brenda Shreve, Red Barn Quilting
www.brendasredbarn.com
99 County Road 2285
Barnsdall, OK 74002
918-847-2544

Wanda Jones, The Tangled Thread
www.thetangledthread.com
230 E. Sixth St.
Pawhuska, OK 74056
918-287-4826

About the Author

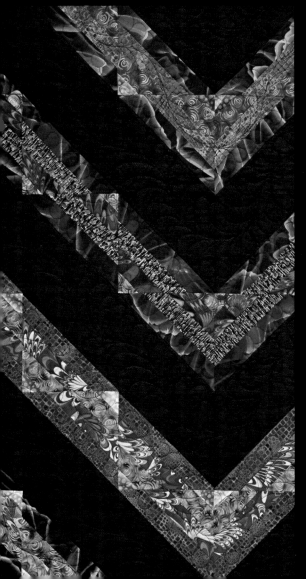

Lerlene Nevaril has been interested in needle arts since the age of five, when her grandmother taught her to make doll clothes on a treadle sewing machine. She went from there to making her own clothes, and then to knitting, embroidery, and needlepoint. In 1979, she picked up a copy of *Quilter's Newsletter* magazine, and she has been quilting ever since.

A desire to have someone else to talk quilting with led her to organize a quilt guild in Sioux City, Iowa, and serve as its first president. In 1988, she served as a regional coordinator for the Iowa Quilt Research Project.

In 1996, with a business partner, Lerlene opened Heart & Hand Dry Goods Co., a quilt shop in Sioux City. In 1999, Heart & Hand was one of the ten shops featured in American Patchwork and Quilting's *Quilt Sampler* magazine.

Lerlene published her first book, *Hidden Block Quilts*, in 2002, and she left her quilt shop the following year to devote more time to traveling and writing. She wrote *Crowning Glories*, another hidden block book, in 2005 and *Over Easy: Creative Ideas for Pieced Quilt Backs* in 2006.

Lerlene has appeared as a guest on *Simply Quilts with Alex Anderson* and has taught and lectured for shops and guilds from Minnesota to Colorado to Florida. She taught at the 2004 Houston Quilt Festival and has had several of her quilts published in *McCall's Quilting* magazine.

Lerlene currently lives in Oklahoma. For more information on her teaching schedule, lectures, and classes, visit her website at

Great Titles *from* C&T PUBLISHING

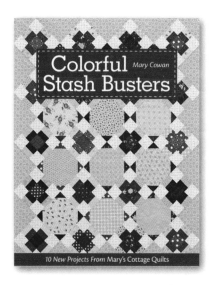

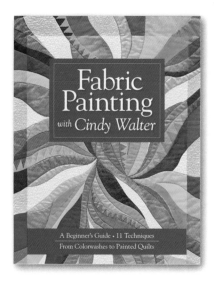

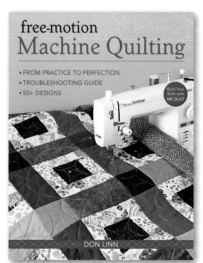

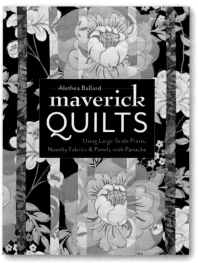

Available at your local retailer or **www.ctpub.com** *or* **800-284-1114**